Animal Legends

Retold by
Carol Watson

Adapted by Gill Harvey

Illustrated by
Nick Price

Reading Consultant: Alison Kelly
University of Surrey Roehampton

Contents

Chapter 1

The cat and
the rat

You might not believe it now,
when cats chase rats and rats
hate cats, but long ago, they
were best friends.

3

One cat
and rat lived
very happily
together on
an island.

The island
had all they
needed. There were birds for
the cat to chase...

...and plenty of
juicy plants for
the rat to
nibble with
her sharp
front teeth.

There was only one problem.
There wasn't much else to do.
Most days they were bored.

Then, one morning, the rat
had an idea.

Why don't we
look for somewhere
else to live?

Purrr-fect! But how
would we get there?

The rat thought about it. How could they leave the island? Then she twitched her whiskers and smiled.

"That's easy," she said.

We'll make a boat from the trunk of a tree!

The rat gnawed at a tree until it toppled over...

Timber!

...and the cat scratched out the inside of the trunk, so they had somewhere to sit.

Finally, the rat nibbled two branches and made them into oars. They were ready to go to sea.

The cat stepped into the boat and took the oars. Then the rat pushed the boat out onto the waves.

"Here goes!" said the cat.

"There's nothing to worry about!" said the rat. "We'll be fine."

They rowed and rowed until it grew dark. The cat was so tired, he fell asleep.

Oh no! We forgot to bring food.

But the rat felt hungry. She

was so hungry, she began to nibble the side of the boat.

But she made such a noise, she woke up the cat.

"Don't worry!" squeaked the rat. "You're dreaming."
So the cat went back to sleep.

The rat was very greedy and kept on gnawing at the boat. Munch... munch... munch...

Suddenly, she stopped.

Oh no! What have I done?

The rat had eaten so much, she'd made a hole in the boat.

Water started to slosh up
through the hole and the boat
began to sink.

The cat woke up with a
start. "I'm wet!" he squealed.

We're sinking!

We'll have to swim!

They had to leap from the boat and swim for their lives.

This is all your fault, rat!

The cat was very angry. He hated getting wet. "I'm going to eat *you* when we get to shore!" he spluttered.

Help!

The rat scrambled up the shore and ran to a sandhill. She dug a hole as fast as she could and dived into it.

Got to dig... got to dig...

The hole was too small for the cat to squeeze into. "I'm safe!" thought the rat.

But the cat didn't give up so easily. He peered into the hole.

"I'll wait for you, rat!" he called. "You'll have to come out sometime."

So, he sat and he waited... and waited...

...and waited. But the rat
never came out.

She dug a tunnel all the way
through the hill and ran out
on the other side.

And that is why, today, a
cat will sit for hour upon hour,
waiting to pounce on a rat.

Chapter 2

Why monkeys live in trees

Many years ago, the king of the jungle was a gorilla named Naresh. All the animals wanted to marry his daughter, but she didn't know who to choose.

One day, Naresh spotted a big wooden barrel sitting on the grass. "That's new!" he said and looked inside.

The barrel was full of greasy water. Naresh took a sip. It tasted of fire. "Fire water?" he said. "That might be useful."

Naresh took the barrel home and called the other animals

together.

"I have a barrel of fire water!" he said. "And it will help us decide who's to marry my daughter."

Whoever can drink the whole barrel may have my beautiful daughter as his bride.

The animals were very excited. Everyone wanted to try. They pushed and shoved closer to the barrel, but the elephant got there first.

"Just watch. This will be easy!" he boasted.

The elephant dipped his trunk into the barrel. He sucked up some fire water and... sneezed.

Ah-chooooo!

"Oww!" he snorted, spraying water everywhere. "It stings! No one could drink that!" And he rushed off.

The hippopotamus tried next. "I live in the river and drink water all the time," he said. "I'm not scared of a bit of fire water!"

So he took a big mouthful...

...and almost choked. He spat out the fire water and ran to the river to cool his mouth.

Next, the warthog stepped forward.

"I can eat or drink anything," he bragged.

No problem!

He drank from the barrel and coughed. "Ugh! That's horrible!" he shouted.

Yeeeuk!

"What fools you are," cried a voice. It was the leopard. "And you're all far too ugly to marry the king's daughter."

I am handsome, and I shall drink the water.

He stepped up to the barrel and just as quickly stepped back again. Even the smell of fire water made him feel sick.

The other animals laughed at the leopard and he crept away in shame. Then a little voice piped up.

It was a tiny monkey. The animals stared at him. How could he drink the water?

Naresh smiled. "You can try if you want," he said. "But you must drink all the water and finish it today."

I don't want a single drop left.

"May I drink a little at a time with rests in between?" asked the monkey.

Naresh was a fair king. "Of course," he said.

So the tiny monkey climbed onto the barrel. The other animals gathered around, grinning. This was going to be funny.

I, Telinga, shall drink the water and marry Naresh's daughter!

But the monkey seemed very sure of himself.

The monkey gulped a large mouthful of the fire water, then ran off into the bushes.

"Where's he going?" the other animals wondered.

After a few moments, the monkey was back. He climbed

up the side of the barrel, took another gulp of fire water...

...and ran off to the bushes, just as he'd done before.

But Telinga, the monkey, had a secret. He wasn't alone. Behind the bushes sat a whole tribe of monkeys, who all looked exactly the same.

Each monkey took turns to drink some of the burning fire water.

By the end of the day, the barrel was empty. The other animals were astonished.

"Now I shall meet my bride," said Telinga proudly.

The monkey stood before the old gorilla. "Well done," said Naresh. "You have completed the task. You may marry my daughter."

But his daughter didn't look too pleased.

I've got to marry *him*?

Ah, my lovely bride!

Suddenly, the giraffe gave a shout. He had seen something interesting.

"Hey!" he cried. "There's a whole tribe of monkeys hiding in the bushes!"

What are you up to?

"Telinga cheated!" roared the animals. "His friends have helped him!"

The monkeys didn't wait to hear any more. They ran off, leaping into the trees to be out of reach.

Monkeys have lived up in trees ever since. They're much too scared to come down.

Chapter 3

The rabbits and the crocodile

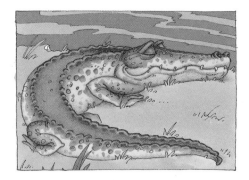

There was once a time when crocodiles lived on land, not in the water. One grumpy old crocodile lived near a river and lazed in the sun all day.

One day, a baby rabbit hopped past, looking for some tasty leaves.

"Hello!" he called and woke up the crocodile. The crocodile was furious.

Go away! I'm trying to sleep!

As the crocodile shut his
eyes again, the rabbit hopped
closer. He had spotted a bunch
of fresh green leaves, just by
the crocodile's nose.

With loud crunching, he
began to gobble them up.

The crocodile's eyes snapped open.

"Get away from those leaves!" he roared. And he snapped at the rabbit with his enormous jaws.

GO AWAY!

The little rabbit ran and ran. He didn't stop until he reached his burrow.

"The crocodile nearly ate me!" he told his mother. "But I didn't do anything wrong."

His mother was very angry. "It's time that crocodile was taught a lesson," she said firmly. "He's grumpy and lazy and it just won't do."

Gathering the other rabbits together, she told them she had a plan.

The next day, the rabbits went into the woods. They collected branches, twigs and leaves and stuffed them into a sack.

"That's enough!" said the rabbit's mother and off they went to find the crocodile.

They didn't have to look far. He was by the riverbank, asleep as usual. The rabbits crept closer.

Sneaking up, they made a big circle of twigs, leaves and branches around the crocodile.

Then the mother rabbit set light to the circle. The fire crackled and spat and smoke billowed up.

The crocodile woke with a jump. When he saw the fire, he bellowed in fear.

The fire was licking at his scales. Taking a flying leap, he jumped right over the flames...

...and disappeared into the river with a splash.

When the crocodile heard the rabbits laughing, he was very annoyed. He shouted at them from the river.

"Keep off our land then!" cried the rabbits and that's how it's stayed ever since.

Try these other books in
Series One:

Dragons: Stan must outwit a hungry
dragon to feed his children. Victor must
persuade two dragons not to eat him. Will
they do it? Read these tales to find out.

Magical Animals: A horse that can fly?
A creature that's half-lion, half-eagle? If
you think they sound amazing, wait until
you see the other animals in this book.

The Dinosaurs Next Door: Stan loves
living next door to Mr. Puff. His house is
full of amazing things. Best of all are the
dinosaur eggs – until they begin to hatch...

The Monster Gang: Starting a gang is
a great idea. So is dressing up like monsters.
But if everyone is in disguise, how do
you know who's who?

Series editor: Lesley Sims

Designed by
Katarina Dragoslavić

First published in 2003 by Usborne Publishing Ltd., Usborne House,
83-85 Saffron Hill, London EC1N 8RT, England. www.usborne.com
Copyright © 2003, 1989,1982 Usborne Publishing Ltd.